Baby animals in rivers

Bobbie Kalman
Crabtree Publishing Company
www.crabtreebooks.com

Created by Bobbie Kalman

For Victor Siemens
I hope you like the cute baby animals
in this book. Which is your favorite animal?

Author and
Editor-in-Chief
Bobbie Kalman

Editor
Kathy Middleton

Proofreader
Crystal Sikkens

Design
Bobbie Kalman
Katherine Berti
Samantha Crabtree
    (front cover)

Photo research
Bobbie Kalman

Print and production coordinator
Katherine Berti

Illustrations
Katherine Berti: p. 6–7 (background), 24 (rivers)
Jeannette McNaughton-Julich: p. 18 (beaver lodge),
    24 (homes)

Photographs
Creatas: p. 12 (bottom)
All other images by Shutterstock

Library and Archives Canada Cataloguing in Publication

Kalman, Bobbie
    Baby animals in river habitats / Bobbie Kalman.

(The habitats of baby animals)
Includes index.
Issued also in electronic formats.
ISBN 978-0-7787-1019-6 (bound).--ISBN 978-0-7787-1033-2 (pbk.)

    1. Stream animals--Infancy--Juvenile literature. 2. Stream
ecology--Juvenile literature. I. Title. II. Series: Kalman, Bobbie.
Habitats of baby animals.

QL145.K34 2013   j591.3'92091693   C2012-907718-6

Library of Congress Cataloging-in-Publication Data

CIP available at the Library of Congress

Crabtree Publishing Company

Printed in Canada/012013/MA20121217

www.crabtreebooks.com   1-800-387-7650

Published in Canada
Crabtree Publishing
616 Welland Ave.
St. Catharines, Ontario
L2M 5V6

Published in the United States
Crabtree Publishing
PMB 59051
350 Fifth Avenue, 59th Floor
New York, New York 10118

Published in the United Kingdom
Crabtree Publishing
Maritime House
Basin Road North, Hove
BN41 1WR

Published in Australia
Crabtree Publishing
3 Charles Street
Coburg North
VIC, 3058

What is in this book?

What is a habitat?

A **habitat** is a natural place where plants grow and animals live. Some habitats are on land, and some are in water. Oceans, lakes, ponds, and rivers are some water habitats. Oceans are made up of **salt water**, which is water that contains a lot of salt. Lakes, ponds, and rivers contain **fresh water**, which does not contain very much salt.

Many kinds of fish and other animals, like this sea turtle, live in ocean habitats. Ocean waters are very salty.

Living things need water

Plants, animals, and people are **living things**.
Living things grow, change, and make new living things.
Air, sunlight, rocks, and soil are **non-living** things.
Water is also a non-living thing. Living things need
water to be healthy and to grow. Plants, animals,
and people cannot live without water.

*This bear and her **cub**, or baby, are living things.*
The plants around them are also living things. The
bears and the plants both need water to stay alive.

What is a river?

A river is a body of water that flows from high places to lower places. As rivers flow, they carry fresh water to plants, animals, and people. All over the world, there are animals that live in rivers or near them. Geese, hippos, otters, alligators, and beavers are just a few of the animals that live in rivers or along their **banks**. A bank is the land at the edge of a river. Many other animals visit rivers to drink fresh water, to find food, and to cool their bodies.

These wolf pups have come to a river for a drink of water.

The **source** of a river is where it begins. The **mouth** is where it ends. Rivers change as they flow from source to mouth. Many rivers flow quickly and roughly down mountains. Some drop over steep rocks at **waterfalls**. Their paths can also wind over land in large curves and bends called **meanders**.

source

waterfall

meander

Streams are small, narrow, shallow rivers.

mouth

7

River babies

Some animals spend all their time in water. Others spend time both in water and on land. These pages show a few of the baby animals that live in or beside rivers.

gosling
(baby goose)

alligator hatchling

cygnet
(baby swan)

crocodile
hatchling

hippo calves

beaver pup

brown bear cub

baby nutria

otter pup

tiger cub

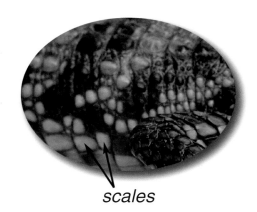
alligator hatchling

scales

Baby reptiles

Reptiles are animals whose bodies are covered in **scales**. Scales are hard bony plates that protect a reptile's body. Alligators, crocodiles, and caimans are reptiles. They live in rivers and in **wetlands** at the edges of rivers. Wetlands are areas that are covered with water for all or part of the year.

Alligators and crocodiles grow inside eggs that their mothers have laid. The babies **hatch**, or break out of the eggs. That is why they are called hatchlings. Baby reptiles look like their parents, but they are much smaller.

crocodile hatchlings

This caiman hatchling finds insects to eat on the plants at the edges of rivers. As an adult, it will eat fish, turtles, birds, and large land animals such as deer.

These baby alligators hatched on land. Their mother carried them to water, but many hatchlings must find their own way to their water homes. Most reptile mothers do not look after their babies.

Mammal mothers

A river otter mother has between one and four pups. The pups drink her milk for about twelve weeks. At nine weeks, she brings the pups fish to eat, as well.

Most reptile mothers do not take care of their babies, but **mammal** mothers do. Mammals are animals with hair or fur. Most mammal mothers feed their babies, keep them safe, and teach them how to survive. The babies drink milk made inside the bodies of their mothers. Drinking mother's milk is called **nursing**.

Tigers spend a lot of time in rivers. They are very good swimmers. This mother tiger is showing her cub how to find fish and turtles to eat.

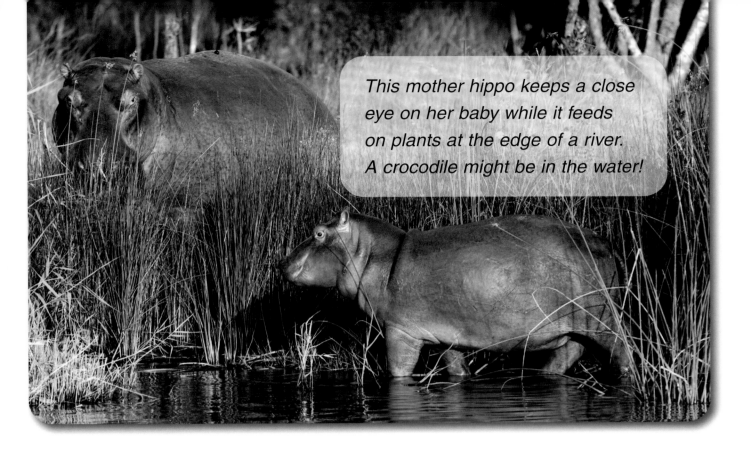

This mother hippo keeps a close eye on her baby while it feeds on plants at the edge of a river. A crocodile might be in the water!

This mother lion brought her cubs to a river for a drink of water.

Baby birds

Birds are animals with wings and feathers. They lay eggs, from which baby birds hatch. Like mammal mothers, most bird mothers take care of their babies. Many bird fathers also help build nests for the babies and bring them food after they hatch.

Both of these swan parents are looking after their cygnets. There are plenty of plants for the birds to eat in the river and on land.

Where do they go?

Birds that live in places with cold winters **migrate**, or travel, to warmer places in autumn. They return in the spring to lay eggs and raise their babies. Some make nests on the banks of rivers and raise their babies both in water and on land.

Canada geese migrating

These Canada geese parents are watching over their goslings, or babies. The goslings will grow quickly and will migrate with their parents when autumn comes.

What do they eat?

Animals find different kinds of foods to eat in rivers and on their banks. Some animals eat mainly plants. Plant-eaters are called **herbivores**. Animals that eat other animals are called **carnivores**. **Predators** are carnivores that hunt other animals for food. The animals they hunt are called **prey**. Animals that eat both plants and other animals are called **omnivores**.

Every evening, this baby hippo comes out of the water to eat the plants that grow on the riverbank. Hippos are herbivores.

Baby crocodiles eat insects and frogs, but as adults, they hunt big animals like this wildebeest. Crocodiles hunt big prey both in rivers and on land.

salmon

This mother bear is catching a salmon that is swimming up a waterfall. Her cub watches and learns. Bears like to eat fish, but they also eat all kinds of plants. They are omnivores.

River homes

Some animals, such as beavers, nutrias, and many birds, make homes on or beside rivers. Beavers build homes, called **lodges**, on slow-moving rivers using mud and sticks. First, they build **dams** to slow down river water and make it still. Under the water, beavers dig tunnels through which they enter their lodge.

Baby beavers are born in the lodge and do not go outside during their first month of life.

Beavers have built two dams on this river.

Baby beavers help their mothers collect sticks for repairing dams and lodges.

burrow

The homes of nutrias are **burrows**, or tunnels, dug into the soft mud on riverbanks. Nutrias can enter their homes from land, as well as from the river.

Some bird mothers, like this swan, build nests on rivers. They use the mud, grasses, and sticks at the edge of the water to make their nests.

Energy in food

Animals need **energy**, or power, to breathe, move, grow, and stay alive. They get their energy from eating plants or other animals. Plants get their energy from the sun. When animals eat the plants, they get the sun's energy, too. The leaves of these water plants grow above water to catch the sun's energy.

sunlight

1. Plants make their own food from air, sunlight, and water. They take in water through their roots. They take in air and sunshine through their leaves, where food is made. Making food from sunlight is called ***photosynthesis****.*

20

A food chain

When an animal eats another animal that has eaten a plant, there is a **food chain**. This river food chain is made up of grasses, a baby hippo, and a crocodile.

2. When a baby hippo eats plants, it receives some of the sun's energy.

3. When a crocodile eats the baby hippo, some of the sun's energy is passed from the plant to the hippo and then to the crocodile.

River babies quiz

How much have you learned about baby animals in rivers? Take this quiz and find out what you know!

river otter

1. Name two kinds of living things and three non-living things in this picture.

2. What is a beaver's home called?

3. This bear cub is a mammal. Name four other mammals shown on these two pages.

4. This tiger cub is a carnivore and predator. Name two other predators that hunt in rivers.

5. Name two kinds of animals that hatch from eggs.

6. What kind of animal is:
a) a gosling?
b) a crocodile?
c) a lion?

gosling

lion cub

crocodile hatchling

Words to know and Index